YOUR KNOWLEDGE HAS VALUE

- We will publish your bachelor's and master's thesis, essays and papers

- Your own eBook and book - sold worldwide in all relevant shops

- Earn money with each sale

Upload your text at www.GRIN.com
and publish for free

Bibliographic information published by the German National Library:

The German National Library lists this publication in the National Bibliography; detailed bibliographic data are available on the Internet at http://dnb.dnb.de .

This book is copyright material and must not be copied, reproduced, transferred, distributed, leased, licensed or publicly performed or used in any way except as specifically permitted in writing by the publishers, as allowed under the terms and conditions under which it was purchased or as strictly permitted by applicable copyright law. Any unauthorized distribution or use of this text may be a direct infringement of the author s and publisher s rights and those responsible may be liable in law accordingly.

Imprint:

Copyright © 2018 GRIN Verlag
Print and binding: Books on Demand GmbH, Norderstedt Germany
ISBN: 9783668966970

This book at GRIN:

https://www.grin.com/document/488890

Jonas Vieracker

A Survey on Healthcare Digitization Accelerating Transformation While Mitigating Data Protection Threats in German Hospitals

GRIN Verlag

GRIN - Your knowledge has value

Since its foundation in 1998, GRIN has specialized in publishing academic texts by students, college teachers and other academics as e-book and printed book. The website www.grin.com is an ideal platform for presenting term papers, final papers, scientific essays, dissertations and specialist books.

Visit us on the internet:

http://www.grin.com/

http://www.facebook.com/grincom

http://www.twitter.com/grin_com

A Survey on Healthcare Digitization: Accelerating Transformation While Mitigating Data Protection Threats in German Hospitals

Jonas Vieracker

Riga Technical University, Rīga, LV-1658, Latvia

Abstract. The digital transformation of the healthcare industry did become a trending topic in Germany of the recent years. Causes for it have been the latest technological developments, Big Data, and the need for medical elucidation of patients. Unfortunately, Germany is not considered to be the pioneer in digitizing medical care in comparison to leading countries in the European Union, although the opportunities are promising. Next to ethical and technical challenges one major threat is created by the high quality of data security, which is required by German and European law, especially starting from 2018, when the new EU General Data Protection Regulation is entering into force. This survey paper will firstly shed a light on opportunities and challenges of healthcare digitization in Germany before elaborating on the detailed root causes of harming the digitalization. The main focus will be to provide high quality data security in hospital IT in line with the applying laws and regulations. Therefore, two approaches by different authors will be assessed and compared.

Keywords: Digital transformation, Healthcare, Hospitals, Germany, Data security, XML, Healthcare information system (HIS)

1 Introduction

Digital transformation is considered to be the industrial revolution of the 21st century. Basically, every industry is affected by the recent technological changes in automation and digitization. Unfortunately, the current state of digitalization heavily differs among Europe. In their Digital Transformation Scoreboard 2017 authors on behalf of the European Commission evaluated European member states according to different metrics regarding the status of digital transformation. Although, Germany is considered to have the "best digital transformation enabling environment" in terms of infrastructure, investments, skills, e-leadership and entrepreneurial culture, it is allocated behind Europe's pioneers[1]. Scandinavia and north-western Europe is leading the field, whereas Germany, once being popular for innovation, is chasing after the expectation. Luckily, not every German industry is lacking in digital progression. While some sectors, such as the producing industry, are heavily investing in the digital change (e.g. Industry 4.0), others did not yet take the chance on benefiting of digital opportunities. According to

Eichhorst et al. [2], almost 60 percent of German hospitals do not have any strategy regarding transforming their processes digitally and only 1.6 percent operate high quality digital processes and business models. An overview of the current state on digital transformation in German hospitals is illustrated by Figure 1 and Figure 2.

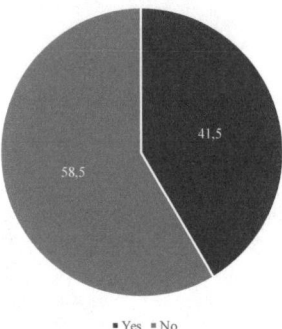

Fig. 1. Existence of Digitization Strategies in German Hospitals (in percent) [2]

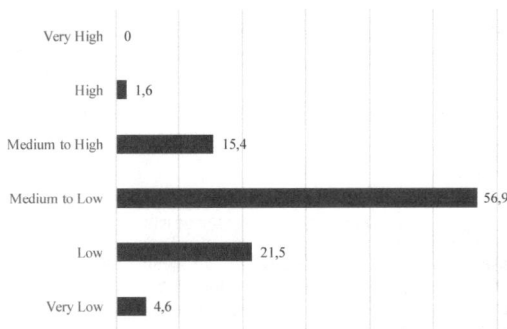

Fig. 2. State and Quality of Digitization in German Hospitals (in percent) [2]

The integral question on this topic is, why the German healthcare sector is still in its infancy regarding digital transformation. What is hindering the change, and which opportunities can be taken by healthcare service providers, especially hospitals? The following survey paper will shed a light on current digitization opportunities and challenges for German hospitals and its regulations. Further, the main focus of this paper will be to analyze facades of data security threats in hospitals and providing potential approaches in order to enhance the quality of data security.

This topic and the corresponding survey paper is based on four pillars, elaborating on each other. These four concepts and associated references are exhibited in Table 1. During the research, digital resources have been considered. Next to online libraries, such as SpringerLink or IEEE Xplore Digital Library, websites of health IT conferences, magazines, and blogs have been considered to supplement the four concepts. Most arguments are based on journals, academic papers, and website/ magazine articles, due to the timeliness of its information. Using current sources is of high importance regarding digitization and data security, as it is a rising phenomenon of the recent years and due to the new Data Protection Regulation of the European Union (EU), which is taking effect in May 2018. Therefore, the website of the European Union, as well as the one of the German Federal Ministry of Health, have been accessed in order to obtain information on the current legislation.

Table 1. Topic concepts and associated references

	Opportunities and Threats of Healthcare Digitization	Healthcare Data Security – Laws and Regulations	Data Security Issues in Hospitals	How to Provide High Quality Data Security
Reference 1	X			
Reference 2	X			
Reference 3	X			
Reference 4	X		X	
Reference 5	X			
Reference 6	X			
Reference 7	X			
Reference 8		X		
Reference 9		X		
Reference 10		X		X
Reference 11		X		
Reference 12			X	
Reference 13			X	
Reference 14			X	
Reference 15				X

2 Opportunities and Challenges of Healthcare Digitization

2.1 Leveraging Healthcare Digitization Opportunities

Opportunities of healthcare digitization are broadly discussed in Germany. When researching for benefits of digital transformation in community health, various experts are exhibiting their own vision on the future of digital health. Nevertheless, these objectives have to be considered with caution, as the technical feasibility of some visions are currently highly doubtful. However, experts already came up with technologies, being easily realizable with the current state of technology and characteristics of healthcare in German hospitals. Lux and Breil [3] elaborate on various opportunities in the field of digitalization in the healthcare industry in the correspondent magazine. Some of their approaches can already be experienced in the industry, while others will characterize the digital future of healthcare. Mobile/ electronic health (eHealth) became, with the rising amount of smartphone and wearable users, a trending topic. It allows patients to gather different kind of health-related information, whereas health service providers, such as insurance companies, hospitals, and doctors can use the data for analytical reasons. Another aspect of mobile health is the electronic health record, which stores patient data digitally next to enabling patients to have control about the usage of their data by others. This is a huge advance to prior times, as the patient can decide, when, where, and who is able to access their sensitive data. Unfortunately, this approach is not yet implemented in Germany, while Scandinavia and the Baltic countries are already making use of the technology. Providing all kinds of medical information digitally also clears the way for Big Data. In their article, Olaronke and Oluwaseun [4] elaborate on the difficulties and benefits of leveraging the power of Big Data in the healthcare industry. Next to classifying medical data, they are also exhibiting practical examples on how to analyze it, before describing limitations and challenges, such as data security, privacy, and integrity. However, once making use of this powerful tool, insurance companies, hospitals, and doctors can benefit immensely. Disease patterns and corresponding treatments can be analyzed at large scales, resulting in more effective and efficient medication planning, according to Lux and Breil [3]. Moving away from digitizing information, processes, such as patient check-in, online appointment planning, etc. can be automated, resulting in increased operational speed and a reduced usage of resources. Further, eLearning technologies can be leveraged to facilitate the professional training of hospital employees, next to their jobs [3]. The more connected the entire healthcare industry becomes, the more efficient all participants can work. Unfortunately, this progress comes at a cost, which will be discussed in the following section.

2.2 Analyzing Healthcare Digitization Challenges

Being excited by the opportunities and benefits of a connected healthcare system, one need to be precautious with potential threats. It contains many challenges, which have been addressed by various experts. The references used for this survey paper are covering the most crucial ones in terms of transformation success. Further, this paper will mostly consider data security threats and how to mitigate them. From a commercial perspective, new business models need to be created in order to afford the high investments on technology. Lux and Breil [3] state, that business models from other industries cannot be easily applied. Generating revenues from data will most healthcare customers hinder to engage in the change, as this is a matter of highly sensitive data. On the other side, and advert-based revenue model creates distrust among the user and is not well received. Solving this issue is also considered to be crucial for the success of healthcare digitization. Moreover, the human factor needs to be handled. Hospitals need to ensure that employees and customers are making use of the systems. Without appropriate usage, projects are doomed to failure. Another shocking aspect of digital transformation is described by Gerald Hörhan. In his book [5] he is tackling the topic of job losses in industries, which are traditional and inflexible, meaning sectors that are reshaped by the digital transformation. Most of organizations within these sectors are also characterized by standardized manual jobs. Although, the hospital sector consists out of academic and non-academic personnel, it is likely to suffer most, amongst others. Even doctors without certain specializations, such as surgery, will be affected by the progress of digital transformation. The following scenario will clarify this argument: by leveraging big data, patterns for simple disease can be easily created. In combination with improved wearable technologies, which monitor a person all time, the "patient" can get information on his disease and which measures should be taken. In case of necessary medication, the wearable will be able to send a prescription request, which will be automatically be declined or approved so that the patient will be able to easily order the medication. In this scenario neither a doctor, nor a nurse or a pharmacist is needed. Taking care of this challenge will also become a tier one priority of a healthcare organization's management next to dealing with technological requirements.

From a technical perspective the lack of standards regarding infrastructure communication and semantics is considered to be a major challenge [2, 3]. In Germany, the law on eHealth is already creating the basis for interoperability within healthcare IT, however governmental organs and industry organizations are forced to elaborate further on the basis to accelerate the transformation [3]. Moreover, the complexity of the IT architecture is a critical success factor for digitizing the industry. The goal in hospital IT is to combine traditional medical systems with new technologies, such as wearables, social media, etc. However, due to the disperse communication and data exchange of systems, this becomes a highly difficult task, which needs to be solved to benefit from the full potential of digital transformation [2, 3]. The biggest challenge of this topic is the area of data security. Medical data is considered to be the most sensitive customer data. The protection from any kind of hazard is the first priority of every medical service provider. Concerns around data protection are either technical or ethical. Technically, high security standards need to be established while from an ethical perspective a transparent access right management describes a possible solution. Only those, who are directly involved in a medical service for a patient are granted access to the relevant data [2, 3, 6]. Ensuring high quality data security will be the focus of this paper. Potential approaches will be exemplified in the fourth concept.

All in all, the mentioned references consider healthcare digitization as indispensable and unstoppable. They are supported by the arguments published in the book of Menville, Audrain-Pntevia, and William [7]. Transforming the hospital industry will lead to higher efficiency in processes, quality, and resource planning, as well as cost savings, although high initial investments are expected. Dealing with and mitigating the threats mentioned by different sources has to be prioritized. Next to innovative business models, hospitals are forced to increase their information technology budgets, as it considered to be the backbone of a hospitals future.

2.3 Healthcare Data Security – Laws and Regulations

When covering the area of data security in Germany, national and European law needs to be considered in order to understand the huge challenges organizations are facing. Especially in the recent years, data security has become a highly discussed topic, due to the vast violations of enterprises, such as Facebook and Google, and regulations in the healthcare sector vary between countries. The personal data these companies are abusing are heavily influencing and limiting the privacy of individuals. Therefore, strict rules need to be set to embank such misuse.

Concerning the healthcare sector data security regulations are even more important, due to the sensibility of medical data. In this paper two major sources will explain the legislation of medical data security. As widely known, the European Union's (EU) new General Data Protection Regulation will take effect on May 15, 2018. This regulation now becomes mandatory for all members of the EU. Examining the changes within the regulation is indispensable for this topic, as it gives valuable insights about the data protection requirements when operating IT systems. As digitization is fostering the integration of traditional and new IT systems, hospitals need to be informed about the impacts of the regulation. According to Lenhard [8] there will be three integral impacts on hospital IT within the new EU regulation. First, data security documentation will be standardized, indicating for the hospitals to check and re-work their data security documentation, especially with regard to order data processing, as hospitals are in possession of multiple versions. Secondly, data security certification for the responsible IT manager are highly recommended as the responsibilities and risks of theses managers will increase [8]. Lastly, the European Union is highly focusing the term "state-of-the-art technology". The regulation is not explicitly instructing on specific IT-security processes solely to avoid changes in the law as soon as a mentioned technology becomes obsolete [8]. This indicates that hospitals need to work with the latest IT security technology in order to avoid fines, which can account up to 4 percent of annual revenue, in case of any security breach or data loss. Finlayson-Brown et. al. [9] describe in their article the changes of the new EU data protection regulation supporting the previously mentioned arguments. They further provide a comprehensive overview about tasks needed to be undertaken in order to operate systems, conform to the regulation. Next to alteration of the General Data Protection Regulation, Asija and Nallusamy [10], mention EU directives, directly considering health care data. Certainly, directives are not as powerful as EU regulations, however in order to avoid potential lawsuits these directives need to be considered, as well.

In addition to European law, Germany adopted a law on "electronic Health" (eHealth) in the beginning of 2016. According to the German Federal Ministry of Health [11], this legislation will encourage and accelerate the digitalization process of healthcare especially doctors' offices and hospitals. The law sets the foundation for the creation of the relevant infrastructure through the provision of guidelines and financial subsidies, while demanding strict compliance concerning data security rules.

In detail, the legislation [11] set the basis for an electronic patient record, which is already used by other member states of the European Union. Until its implementation in 2018 it is represented as an eHealth ID card, which stores sensitive patient data.

Further, through an ongoing integration within the healthcare sector, it will also be possible to automatize the creation of medication plans, facilitating the anamnesis of and medication prescription of doctors, leading to less reciprocal effects. In addition, staring 2019 an online portal for patients will be available, allowing them to control their data and to add additional information, such as daily blood sugar values in case of being contracted with diabetes. Lastly, the regulation created also the foundation for ongoing development in telemedicine, making it part of common healthcare practices.

With regard to data security, the German Federal Ministry of Health [11] relies on a two-factor-authentication. This security measure requires the official healthcare ID of a doctor, stored within the card reader, and the patient's eHealth ID card including a personal identification number (PIN). This ensures that only doctors, medical staff, and the patient himself have access to the sensitive data. In addition, the last 50 accesses are stored on the ID card to enable a detailed traceability. Unfortunately, the ministry is not providing information on data security with regard to the planned activities in 2018 and 2019. Therefore, monitoring the developments in both, European and national law, is indispensable for hospitals and other medical institutions.

2.4 Data Security Issues in Hospitals

According to Masrom and Rahimly [12] the main purpose of data security in hospital information systems is to achieve patient safety and privacy. They define safety as providing the patient and medical staff with the most accurate information at the right time, whereas privacy characterizes the measurements of protecting the sensitive data from unauthorized access [12]. This concept represents the root causes of data security problems in hospitals. Based on these causes a technical approach to enhance data security will be exhibited in paragraph 2.5 rather than strategic response plans, such as integrity maintenance plan and disaster recovery plan.

Olaronke and Oluwaseun [4] are dividing the causes nourishing data security problems in hospitals as follows. The presence of *fragmentation in healthcare data and systems* is resulting in different security standards and interoberability capabilities, harming the possibilities of data security standards. An exchange of outdated systems would be reasonable, however not affordable, due to high cost. On top of fragmented systems, the hospital IT department as well as management often lacks in know-how, making it even more difficult to progress. In addition, current technological characteristics, such as using XML for data exchange, are causing problems with regard to data security. This topic will be discussed within the fourth concept of this review. Furthermore, Masrom and Rahimly [12] state, that hospitals are facing several changes related to storing, sharing, and distributing health data, due to the fact that hospitals still rely on manual methods, including pen, paper, and the human memory. These manual approaches are not suitable in the age of digitization and form another aspect, that needs to be taken care of, in order to ensure a high degree of data integrity and data security. Further, the *defiance of standards* by medical organizations is a huge burden when applying standardized data security approaches. Standards are created to allow disperse systems, tools, technologies, and platforms to work together. However, hospitals do not comply to many standards regarding information technology [4] .

Lastly, *ethcial challenges* increase the complexity of data security and integrity. Ethics in healthcare is an extremely complicated topic. Detailed user management strategies, meaning who has access to what, when, and how, need to be created in order to ensure ethical compliance [4]. This argument is also supported in the journal of Masrom and Rahimly [12].

Unfortunately, such projects also demand many financial and human resources, which hospitals are currnetly not willed to spend on information technology (IT). All these issues are mainly caused by the lack of financial investments into hospital IT. According to Grätzel von Grätz [13], investments into hospital IT are mostly made if costs are reduced, risks minimized, or organizational improvements achieved. The third cause is hard to measure and difficult to sell to the management, meaning as long as no costs or risks are reduced, investments into hospital IT are rarely considered. A study of McKinsey [14] also supports the increasing demand for investments into a hospital's IT infrastructure in order to cope with the challenges of medical digitization and data security issues. As this paragraph points out, hospitals face many challenges with regard to data security. The complexity and heterogeneity of their systems paired with growing influence of new technologies, such as mobile devices and eHealth, impede the development of a holistically integrated hospital information system, which is capable of communicating with third parties, such as insurance companies. Nevertheless, the development of such a system should be the priority of the healthcare system in the upcoming years in order to leverage the opportunities of digitization.

2.5 How to Provide High Quality Data Security

The research outcome of this paper should be the delivery of better data security in the healthcare and especially hospital sector. Next to the requirement for tremendous additional investments, technological challenges need to be handled. Therefore, two possible approaches will be briefly discussed.

Data-Centric Approach.

The first approach considers a XML based security technology, which is ensuring security standards in terms of access rights, according to country or institution policies. Asija and Nallusamy [10] state that XML is the de facto standard for electronic data exchange around the world. Hospitals do also rely on this data format. The simplicity and richness of its data structure are highly beneficial to its users. However, the possibility that a XML file is manipulated during exchange still exists, which brings unique challenges to the administrator of medical data. Therefore, XML must be enriched with certain security and control mechanisms to ensure a high standard of data security. In their conference proceedings, the authors [10] describe different XML security technologies:

1. XML Digital Signature: lock and seal contents of a document
2. XML Encryption: encryption of contents of an XML element
3. XML Key Management (XKMS): protocol for public key registration, location, and validation

4. Security Assertion Markup Language (SAML): conveying authentication, authorization and attribute assertion
5. XML Access Control Markup Language (XACML): defining access control rules

Unfortunately, according to the authors [10] these technologies are not scalable enough to cope with the requirements of emerging technologies, such as cloud computing. Therefore, they proposed their own model, which differentiate itself from existing solutions. In their research, Asija and Nallusamy [10] found solutions, which are based on an approach in which security levels are defined outside the document by means of an XPATH expression. This definition of security levels at run-time heavily depends on the discretion of the owner, who is granting the privileges to users, which may lead to a non-uniformity of access for users with the same role within an organization. Moreover, the method relies on mechanisms of inheritance for assigning security levels to parent and child nodes, which may lead to ambiguous results and loss of security and privacy of data. Taken these burdens into account, Asija and Nallusamy developed the following model. First, the security levels are attached to the XML schema during design time. Further, the permissions for a particular user to a particular data are mapped during run-time, leading to a uniform access by the end user and a higher security for medical data. Their approach differentiates itself from other work that each node is independent from its parent node, which enables the assignment of individual security levels to each node. In addition, the authors designed a mapping algorithm, which is capable of checking different security levels of data and grants access to users with same or higher security clearance [10]. A detailed representation of the model's proposed XML Schema and the functionality of the algorithm is reserved for further investigation on the topic, as this survey paper should only give a brief overview of the model's functionality. Nevertheless, when analyzing this approach, the authors came up with various advantages. Firstly, the security levels are defined during run-time within the XML Schema and permission of access/ updated/ delete are given at runtime using a mapping algorithm. Secondly, the authors' model differentiate data according to its sensitivity, as every node is assigned an independent security level. Thirdly, high security when exchanging data with other hospitals is ensured, as an user with the respective security level is necessary to access the data. However, the receiving institution would be obliged to conform to the same XML Schema and security levels in order to make use of the data. This again requires standards, which are hard to enforce in healthcare, as already discussed before. Fourthly, the model is operation independent and can be used for read-and-write operations. Fifthly, the data model is flexible and portable, as it can be easily adapted to the respective security standards of different countries or institutions by simply changing the XML Schema without changing the hard-code [10]. Lastly, it is easily realizable, due to the fact that XML is a standard in data transfer and only an adaption of the schema is necessary. All in all, this model provides a profound solution to offer higher data security at hospitals against internal, as well as external threats. Unfortunately, it requires standards for the entire industry to ensure the interoperability of the model between different institutions.

Storage-Centric Approach.
The storage-centric approach was developed as a result of the emerging attacks on patient data and hospital information systems, such as WannaCry [15]. Puppala et. al. [15] already include the vulnerabilities of newest technologies, as mobile health and electronic patient records, deliver high information gains when analyzed correctly, however need to be secured appropriately. In their paper, they propose a security and privacy model implemented in Methodist Environment for Translational and Outcomes Research (METEOR). It was developed at Houston Methodist Hospital and consists of two components: the enterprise data warehouse (EDW) and a software intelligence and analytics (SIA) layer [15]. Puppala et. al. [15] state that this model indicates that patient privacy is best protected by implementing a systematic mix of technologies and best practices such as technical de-identification of data, restrictive data access, and security measures in the underlying technical platforms. Further, the approach of creating a centric data warehouse facilitates securing the underlying data. In addition, a high degree of data security is reached by setting up an end-to-end security, ranging from extraction of data from disparate sources, its transportation towards the data warehouse, potential distribution to data marts or analytics servers, to the final distribution to end-users. Moreover, a two-factor authentication will secure a correct access to the respective data [15].

All in all, this approach is dealing with improving an existing data warehouse. By taking a systematic approach the authors [15] were able to improve the data security of a hospital data warehouse by means of the previous mentioned Software Intelligence and Analytics layer and other mechanisms. This method is a highly practical approach and its feasibility needs to be analyzed at other institutions. However, the feasibility study is reserved for further investigations.

3 Conclusion

The digital transformation and its current opportunities and challenges is unstoppable and will reshape or even reengineer every industry. A central point within the progress will be the availability of high quality data and IT security in order to avoid hacker attacks, such as identity theft or denial-of-service (DoS) threats. This survey paper highlights general opportunities within the fourth industrial revolution, but also sheds a light on the threats organizations in the healthcare industry will face. It is a healthcare institution's first priority to mitigate those risks in order to provide state of the art services and to leverage the full potential of this unique change. The paper also criticizes the current legislation of the European Union and Germany in terms of healthcare digitalization. It is indispensable for the industry to have strict guidelines, as well as support by the respective government organs, as legislation is an additional accelerator of digital healthcare. Fortunately, the increasing pressure Germany is experiencing through the advancements of leading healthcare countries is forcing the government towards additional measures. The focus of this survey paper was the assessment of data security threats in hospitals and the exhibition of potential approaches to solve them. Both models show advantages and disadvantages and cannot be compared on the same level.

With regard to securing information on data level, the first approach is of high value, due to its flexibility. Considering the security of storing and distributing data, the second model is a good starting point. Nevertheless, with regard to storage and distribution, further models need to be assessed in the ongoing research in order to provide alternatives depending on the technical state of the respective hospital. All in all, the underlying survey paper provides detailed information on the research problem. By further analyzing, especially the technical feasibility of the considered approaches and by assessing additional models, a profound solution to the research question can be provided.

References

1. Probst, L., Pedersen, B., Lonkeu, O.-K., Martinez-Diaz, C., Araujo, L.N., PwC, Klitou, D., Conrads, J., Rasmussen, M.: Digital Transformation Scoreboard 2017: Evidence of positive outcomes and current opportunities for EU businesses. (2017)
2. PD Dr. med. Eichhorst, S., Erk, N., Dr. Hehner, S., Dr. Moder, S., Dr. Mohr, N., Dr. Möller, M.: DIGITALISIERUNG IN DEUTSCHEN KRANKENHÄUSERN - Eine Chance mit Milliardenpotenzial für das Gesundheitssystem. (2017)
3. Lux, T., Breil, B., Dörries, M., Gensorowsky, D., Greiner, W., Pfeiffer, D., Rebitschek, F.G., Gigerenzer, G., Wagner, G.G.: Digitalisierung im Gesundheitswesen – zwischen Datenschutz und moderner Medizinversorgung. Wirtschaftsd. - Zeitschrift für Wirtschaftspolitik. 2017, 687–703 (2017)
4. Olaronke, I., Oluwaseun, O.: Big data in healthcare: Prospects, challenges and resolutions. In: 2016 Future Technologies Conference (FTC). pp. 1152–1157. IEEE (2016)
5. Hörhan, G.: Der Stille Raub - Wie das Internet die Mittelschicht zerstört und was Gewinner der digitalen Revolution anders machen. edition a, Wien (2017)
6. Menzel, H.-J.: Papierloses Krankenhaus --- gläserner Patient? Datenschutz und Datensicherheit - DuD. 33, 390 (2009). doi:10.1007/s11623-009-0099-y
7. Menvielle, L., Audrain-Pntevia, A.-F., William, M.: The Digitization of Healthcare New Challenges and Opportunities. Presented at the (2017)
8. Lenhard, T.H.: Die Europäische Datenschutzgrundverordnung - Auswirkungen auf den Datenschutz in Kliniken, http://www.medizin-edv.de/ARCHIV/Praxisleitfaden_kl.pdf, (2016)
9. Finlayson-Brown, J., Et.al.: The EU General Data Protection Regulation, http://www.allenovery.com/SiteCollectionDocuments/Radical changes to European data protection legislation.pdf
10. Asija, R., Nallusamy, R.: Data model to enhance the security and privacy of healthcare data. In: 2014 IEEE Global Humanitarian Technology Conference - South Asia Satellite (GHTC-SAS). pp. 237–244. IEEE (2014)
11. German Federal Ministry of Health: Fragen und Antworten zur elektronischen Gesundheitskarte und zum E-Health-Gesetz | Bundesgesundheitsministerium, https://www.bundesgesundheitsministerium.de/service/begriffe-von-a-z/e/e-health-gesetz/faq-e-health-gesetz.html

12. Masrom, M., Rahimly, A.: Overview of Data Security Issues in Hospital Information Systems. Ailar Pacific Asia J. Assoc. Inf. Syst. Pacific Asia J. Assoc. Inf. Syst. 7, 51–66 (2015)
13. Grätzel von Grätz, P.: E-HEALTH-COM: IT-Investitionen im Krankenhaus, http://e-health-com.de/thema-der-woche/it-investitionen-im-krankenhaus/96fa3e2ed1f62c86aa98a6e5363bf5bf/
14. Laflamme, F.M., Pietraszek, W.E., Rajadhyax, N. V.: Reforming hospitals with IT investment | McKinsey & Company, https://www.mckinsey.com/industries/healthcare-systems-and-services/our-insights/reforming-hospitals-with-it-investment
15. Puppala, M., He, T., Yu, X., Chen, S., Ogunti, R., Wong, S.T.C.: Data security and privacy management in healthcare applications and clinical data warehouse environment. In: 2016 IEEE-EMBS International Conference on Biomedical and Health Informatics (BHI). pp. 5–8. IEEE (2016)

YOUR KNOWLEDGE HAS VALUE

- We will publish your bachelor's and master's thesis, essays and papers

- Your own eBook and book - sold worldwide in all relevant shops

- Earn money with each sale

Upload your text at www.GRIN.com
and publish for free